BRAIN G

Age-Proof Your Brain!

Puzzle Constructors: Michael Adams; Cihan Altay; Philip Carter; Don Cook; Josie Faulkner; Erich Friedman; Dave Green; Luke Haward; Marilynn Huret; Kate Mepham; David Millar; Ellen F. Pill, Ph.D.; Pete Sarjeant; Paul Seaburn; Fraser Simpson; Terry Stickels; Howard Tomlinson

Illustrators: Helem An; Shavan R. Spears

ISBN-13: 978-1-60553-017-8
ISBN-10: 1-60553-017-4

Manufactured in China.

8 7 6 5 4 3 2 1

Honeycomb

There are 14 numbers in the honeycomb below that are surrounded by different numbers (no numbers are repeated around them). Can you find them all?

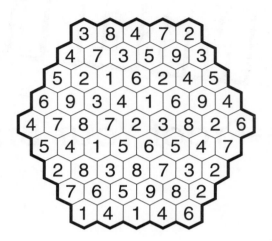

Number Diamonds

The numbers in the center of each figure have been placed using a certain logic. See if you can find the pattern and put the correct number in the final figure.

2 6
⟨48⟩
1 7

9 8
⟨75⟩
3 5

4 2
⟨63⟩
7 8

6 5
⟨48⟩
2 3

7 9
⟨ — ⟩
8 9

Answers on page 28.

Vex-a-gon

Place the numbers 1 through 6 into the triangles of each hexagon. The numbers may be in any order, but they do not repeat within each hexagon shape.

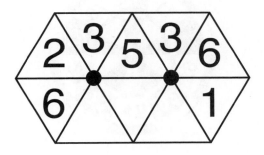

Who's Watching?

I set both my wife's watch and my watch at midnight. Later, I discovered that one of the watches went 2 minutes per hour too slow, and the other went one minute per hour too fast. When I looked at them later the same day, the faster one was exactly one hour ahead of the other.

What was the correct time when I looked at the watches?

Answers on page 28.

Perfect Score

Make 3 successful hits so that the sum of the numbers adds up to 100. Double and triple scores do not apply. Numbers may be used more than once.

Twenty-four Jumble

Arrange the numbers and signs in this cornucopia to come up with the number 24.

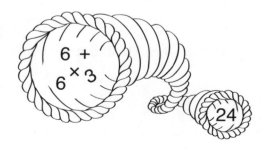

Answers on page 28.

Hitori

The object of this puzzle is to have numbers appear only once in each row and column. By shading a number cell, you are effectively removing that number from its row and column. There's a catch though: Shaded number cells are never adjacent to one another in a row or column.

5	1	5	7	5	4	8	1
6	4	7	8	3	1	2	5
6	8	2	6	4	5	5	5
8	7	1	8	5	2	5	6
5	5	7	4	2	6	7	3
1	5	5	2	3	8	1	4
7	6	3	7	1	5	4	4
6	2	4	1	1	3	6	7

Answer on page 28.

Calcu-doku

Use arithmetic and deductive logic to complete the grid so that each row, each column, and each irregular shape contains the numbers 1 through 4 in some order. Numbers in each outlined set of squares combine to produce the number in the top corner using the mathematical sign indicated. The solution is unique.

1-		2	3+
5+	12×		
	6×		
3+		7+	

Trivia on the Brain

"Wuji" (Number 0), in the Mystical Numbers of Taoism, represents the Null, the Chaos, the Origin, and the End.

Answer on page 28.

Number Crossword

Fill in this crossword with numbers instead of letters. Use the clues to determine which number from 1 through 9 belongs in each empty square. No zeros are used.

1	2		■	3	4
5		6			
■	7				■
8				9	
10		■	11		

ACROSS
- 1. A multiple of 11
- 3. A square number
- 5. Consecutive digits, descending
- 7. A square number
- 8. Consecutive odd digits, in some order
- 10. Digits add up to 4
- 11. A prime number

DOWN
- 1. A multiple of 3
- 2. A palindrome whose digits add up to 18
- 3. Consecutive odd digits, ascending
- 4. An even number
- 6. Consecutive digits, out of order
- 8. A multiple of 7
- 9. An odd number

Answers on page 28.

7

Hashi

Each circle represents an island, with the number inside indicating the number of bridges connected to it. Draw bridges between islands using the number given. There can be no more than 2 bridges going in the same direction, and there must be a continuous path connecting all islands. Bridges can only be vertical or horizontal and may not cross islands or other bridges. We've drawn some bridges to get you started.

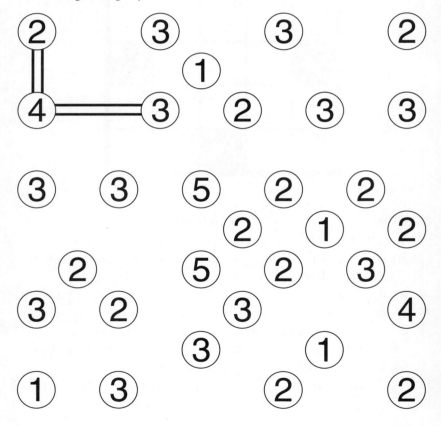

Answer on page 28.

Odd-Even Logidoku

The numbers 1 to 9 appear once in every row, column, long diagonal, irregular shape, and 3 by 3 grid. Cells marked with the letter E contain even numbers. From the numbers given, can you complete the puzzle?

Age Quandary

In 12 years' time, the combined age of my 4 nieces will be 94. What will it be in 5 year's time?

Answers on page 29.

1-2-3

Take the numbers 1, 2, and 3 and place them in the circles below. The challenge is to have only these 3 numbers in each row—no number should repeat. Any combination is allowed.

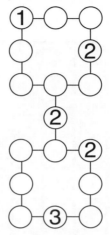

Friendly Pick Up

Best friends Speedy and Pokey started their own bicycle package pick-up service, catering to the businesses that lined both sides of the street they lived on. With each side of the street having the same number of businesses, they decided the best plan would be for Speedy to pick up on one side and Pokey to pick up on the other. In the excitement of the first day, Pokey got his bike turned around and picked up packages at the first 5 businesses on Speedy's side of the street. That's when Speedy caught up to him and took over, so Pokey crossed the street and started visiting the businesses on his side. Living up to his name, Speedy finished the pick-ups on his side and crossed over to help Pokey, making the pick-ups at the last 9 businesses on Pokey's side of the street. How many more pick-ups did Speedy make than Pokey?

Answers on page 29.

Cross-Math

Place the digits 1 through 9 in the empty white squares so that the 3 horizontal and 3 vertical equations are true. Each digit will be used once. Calculations are done from left to right and from top to bottom.

	+		÷		=	2
×		+		+		
	+		+		=	21
×		-		×		
	+		+		=	12
=		=		=		
21		4		20		

Name Calling

Decipher the encoded words in the quip below using the numbers and letters on the phone pad. Remember that each number can stand for 3 or 4 possible letters.

The 9–6–7–7–8 wheel 7–7–8–3–2–5–7 the 5–6–8–3–3–7–8.

1	2 ABC	3 DEF
4 GHI	5 JKL	6 MNO
7 PQRS	8 TUV	9 WXYZ
	0	

Answers on page 29.

Sudoku

Use deductive logic to complete the grid so that each row, each column, and each 3 by 3 box contains the numbers 1 through 9 in some order. The solution is unique.

2					7		4	5
	5	2				7	1	
	6	5					2	9
		6						4
5	1	4	3		9	2	6	7
9					2			
6	4				1	5		
	5	2			4	1		
3	8		7					2

Vex-a-gon

Place the numbers 1 through 6 into the triangles of each hexagon. The numbers may be in any order, but they do not repeat within each hexagon shape.

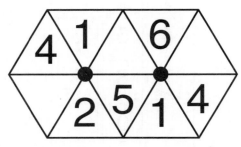

Answers on page 29.

Crypto-logic

Each of the numbers in the sequence below represents a letter. Use the mathematical clues to determine which number stands for which letter and reveal the encrypted word.

Hint: Remember that a / indicates "divided by" and that all sums in parentheses must be done first.

732913247

Clues:

The combined value of all the instances of the numbers that repeat in this encryption is equal to the value of $(Q + 14)$.

$Q = D + S + 1$

$2D = Q + E$

$S = \frac{1}{3} Q$

The repeated number you still don't know the letter for represents I.

I squared equals G.

$Q - G = U$

Miss You Already

What is the missing number in each of the following sets?

A. 13 19 14 17 15 15 16 13 17 11 18 9 ____

B. 7 10 19 13 9 24 ____ 16 12 6 15 18

C. 1 1 8 81 1,024 15,625 ____

Answers on pages 29–30.

Star Power

Fill in each of the empty squares in the grid so that each star is surrounded by the numbers 1 through 8 with no repeats.

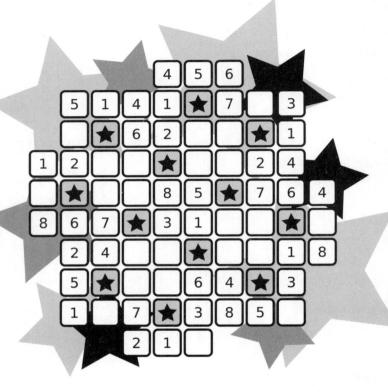

Trivia on the Brain

Albert Einstein's brain weighed 1,230 grams—far below the average brain weight of 1,400 grams.

Answer on page 30.

Number Crossword

Fill in this crossword with numbers instead of letters. Use the clues to determine which of the numbers 1 through 9 belongs in each square. No zeros are used.

ACROSS

1. The sum of its digits is 9

4. Consecutive digits, descending

5. A multiple of 11

6. A multiple of 11

7. Consecutive digits, descending

9. A square number

DOWN

1. Two different digits

2. A palindrome

3. A power of 2

4. A palindrome

5. Three different digits

8. A multiple of 7

Answers on page 30.

Go Figure

Fill each square in the grid with a digit from 1 through 9. When the numbers in each row are added, you will arrive at the total in the right-hand column. When the numbers in each column are added, you will arrive at the total on the bottom line. The numbers in each corner-to-corner diagonal must add up to the totals in the upper and lower right corners.

						28
9	6	2			3	25
	2	2		1		21
	7		2		4	25
2		9	5	3		24
1		2	5	4	2	21
	1		4	8	3	27
26	27	26	21	23	20	29

The Whys and Wherefores

If X and Y are different positive digits, the value of Y could then be from 2 to what number?

$$Y4$$
$$Y8$$
$$+\,X6$$
$$\overline{148}$$

Answers on page 30.

Cross Count

In the chart below, all the letters of the alphabet have been given a value. Fill in the grid with common English terms so that the rows and columns add up correctly.

```
1  2  3  4  5  6  7  8  9

A  B  C  D  E  F  G  H  I

J  K  L  M  N  O  P  Q  R

S  T  U  V  W  X  Y  Z
```

	H			7	17
P			9		27
			5	1	8
N			R	9	20
14	20	16	22		

Trivia on the Brain

Your brain allows you to differentiate between 3,000 and 10,000 distinct smells. Who "nose" if you'd be able to smell anything at all without it!

Answer on page 30.

Sudoku

Use deductive logic to complete the grid so that each row, each column, and each 3 by 3 box contains the numbers 1 through 9 in some order. The solution is unique.

		1			6			7
7	9			1	4			5
6		8	2				9	
1			7	9			6	
	6			3	2			1
	3				1	4		6
4			3	8			5	2
5			6			7		

Twenty-four Jumble

Arrange the numbers and signs in this cornucopia to come up with the number 24.

Answers on page 30.

Perfect Score

Make 3 successful hits so that the sum of the numbers adds up to 100. Double and triple scores do not apply. Numbers may be used more than once.

Number Crossword

Fill in this crossword with numbers instead of letters. Use the clues to determine which of the numbers 1 through 9 belongs in each square. No zeros are used.

ACROSS

1. A square number
4. The sum of its first 2 digits equals the sum of its last 2 digits
6. A palindrome
8. Consecutive digits, descending

DOWN

1. A multiple of 11
2. Consecutive even digits, ascending
3. A square number
5. Consecutive odd digits, ascending
7. 1-Down plus 40

Answers on page 31.

Figuring Fast Food

Fast Food Frank stopped in a brand-new burger joint for his fast food lunch. Checking the lighted menu behind the counter, he saw that the following combinations were available:

Burger and fries: $3.50

Fries and a small drink: $2.25

Small drink and a cookie: $1.50

Burger and a cookie: ***

Unfortunately, the lights behind the price of Frank's favorite combo, a burger and a cookie, were burned out, and he didn't know how much it was. It was the counter clerk's first day on the job, and he didn't know the price either. Luckily, Fast Food Frank was fast at figures and figured out how much the burger and cookie combo costs just by looking at the other combo prices.

How much did he pay?

Trivia on the Brain
On Pi Day (March 14) in 1879, a baby was born in Germany whose name meant "one stone." The baby? None other than Albert Einstein.

Answer on page 31.

Greedy Gears

Place a number between the spokes of each gear so that numbers across from each other add up to the number in the center of the gear. Numbers must also follow the rules on the gear spokes concerning greater than or less than symbols. In the spaces where the spokes of Gear 6 are within the gaps of the other gears, the digit is 6. Duplicate digits may be used more than once on the same gear if necessary but may not be placed next to each other.

Answer on page 31.

Crypto-Logic

Each of the numbers in the sequence below represents a letter. Use the mathematical clues to determine which number stands for which letter and reveal the encrypted word.

Hint: Remember that a / indicates "divided by" and that all sums in parentheses must be done first.

812563

Clues:

$T = 12$

$\frac{1}{3} T = (P - 1)$

$2P = O$

$O - 2 = S$

$O - S = M$

$M / 2 = I$

$M + I = E$

$2E = L$

Calcu-doku

Use arithmetic and deductive logic to complete the grid so that each row, each column, and each irregular shape contains the numbers 1 through 4 in some order. Numbers in each outlined set of squares combine to produce the number in the top corner using the mathematical sign indicated. The solution is unique.

7+	6×	1	2×
		2/	
3-			1-
2	4+		

Answers on page 31.

22

Number Square

Each lettered box in the grid contains a number from 1 through 9. Use the clues to put the digits in their proper places. Each number is used only once.

CLUES

1. The top row contains only digits that are odd prime numbers

2. The middle row contains only digits that are square numbers

3. C + E = G

4. The digits in A, F, B, and I are in consecutive order, ascending

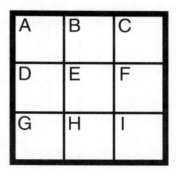

Vex-a-gon

Place the numbers 1 through 6 into the triangles of each hexagon. The numbers may be in any order, but they do not repeat within each hexagon shape.

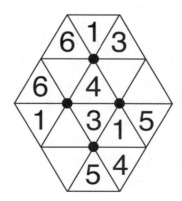

Answers on page 31.

Digital Sudoku

Fill in the grid with digits from 1 through 6 so that in each row, each column, and in each 2 by 3 block each digit appears exactly once. Numbers are in digital form, and some segments have already been filled in.

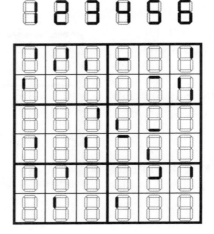

How Much?

Four veteran players from each of the local professional sports teams were at their favorite sports bar arguing about how much they signed for in their rookie years. The bartender was hoping to become a sports agent someday, so he offered to guess their rookie-year salaries. The veterans wrote their rookie salaries on a piece of paper: $8 million, $14 million, $12 million, $10 million. The point guard said he signed for the most. LeBucks signed for more than Peydey, and the pitcher signed for more than Jacques, the goalie. Lefty refused to give a hint about his rookie salary. Peydey the quarterback did not sign for $10 million and neither did Jacques. Can you help the bartender figure out what position each of the pros plays and what their rookie-year salaries were?

Answers on page 31.

Hashi

Each circle represents an island, with the number inside indicating the number of bridges connected to it. Draw bridges between islands using the number given. There can be no more than 2 bridges going in the same direction, and there must be a continuous path connecting all islands. Bridges can only be vertical or horizontal and may not cross islands or other bridges. We've drawn some bridges to get you started.

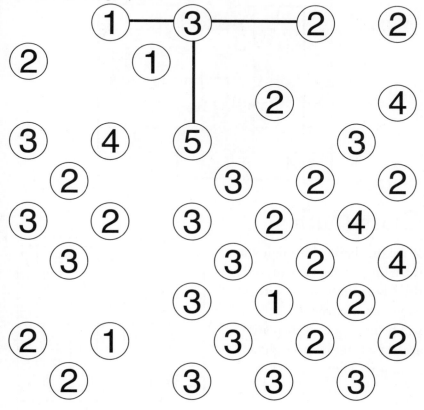

Answer on page 32.

Odd-Even Logidoku

The numbers 1 through 9 appear once in every row, column, long diagonal, 3 by 3 grid, and irregular shape. Cells marked with the letter E contain even numbers. From the numbers already given, can you complete the puzzle?

Cross-Math

Place the digits 1 through 9 in the empty white squares so that the 3 horizontal and 3 vertical equations are true. Each digit will be used once. Calculations are done from left to right and from top to bottom.

	×		+		=	17
+		+		+		
	×		+		=	18
-		-		÷		
	×		+		=	19
=		=		=		
5		2		3		

Answers on page 32.

1-2-3

Take the numbers 1, 2, and 3 and place them in the circles below. The challenge is to have only these 3 numbers in each row—no number should repeat. Any combination is allowed.

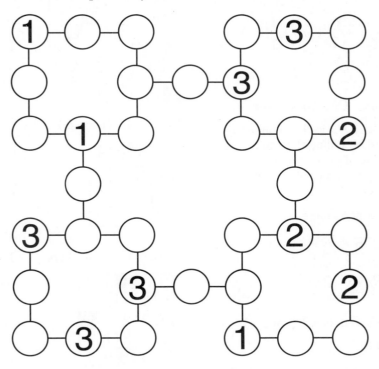

Trivia on the Brain
The world's first calculator, developed in 1967 by Texas Instruments, weighed 55 pounds and cost $2,500!

Answer on page 32.

ANSWERS

. . . .

Honeycomb (page 2)

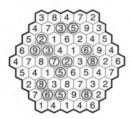

Number Diamonds (page 2)

The number in the diamond is found by adding the 4 numbers outside of the diamond and multiplying their sums by 3 for the answer: 99

Vex-a-gon (page 3)

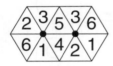

Who's Watching? (page 3)

8 ı Ñ Ñì

As the faster watch gains on the slower one by 3 minutes per hour, it will be exactly 1 hour ahead after 20 hours (20 × 3 = 60).

Perfect Score (page 4)

1+11+88=100

Twenty-four Jumble (page 4)

6 × 3 + 6 = 24

Hitori (page 5)

5	1	5	7	5	4	8	1
6	4	7	8	3	1	2	5
6	8	2	6	4	5	5	5
8	7	1	8	5	2	5	6
5	5	7	4	2	6	7	3
1	5	5	2	3	8	1	4
7	6	3	7	1	5	4	4
6	2	4	1	1	3	6	7

Calcu-doku (page 6)

3	4	2	1
1	3	4	2
4	2	1	3
2	1	3	4

Number Crossword (page 7)

3	3		1	6
6	5	4	3	2
	2	2	5	
9	5	3	7	1
1	3		9	7

Hashi (page 8)

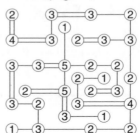

Odd-Even Logidoku (page 9)

9	6	3	7	5	2	4	1	8
4	2	8	3	1	9	6	5	7
1	5	7	6	8	4	3	9	2
3	7	2	5	6	1	8	4	9
6	1	5	9	4	8	2	7	3
8	4	9	2	7	3	5	6	1
5	3	6	8	9	7	1	2	4
2	9	1	4	3	6	7	8	5
7	8	4	1	2	5	9	3	6

Age Quandary (page 9)

66

Combined age in 12 years = 94.

$4 \times 12 = 48$, therefore, combined age now is 94 - 48 = 46

In 5 years time the combined age is, therefore, $46 + 20 (4 \times 5) = 66$

1-2-3 (page 10)

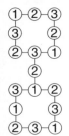

Friendly Pick Up (page 10)

If the number of businesses on each side of the street is X, Speedy picks up X - 5 + 9, or X + 4, while Pokey picks up at 5 + X - 9, or X - 4, making the difference 8. So no matter how many businesses are on the street, Speedy made 8 more pick-ups than Pokey.

Cross-Math (page 11)

3	+	5	÷	4	=	2
×		+		+		
7	+	8	+	6	=	21
×		-		×		
1	+	9	+	2	=	12
=		=		=		
21		4		20		

Name Calling (page 11)

The worst wheel squeaks the loudest.

Sudoku (page 12)

2	3	8	1	9	7	6	4	5
4	9	5	2	6	3	7	1	8
1	7	6	5	4	8	3	2	9
8	2	7	6	1	5	9	3	4
5	1	4	3	8	9	2	6	7
9	6	3	4	7	2	8	5	1
6	4	9	8	2	1	5	7	3
7	5	2	9	3	4	1	8	6
3	8	1	7	5	6	4	9	2

Vex-a-gon (page 12)

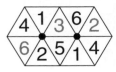

Crypto-logic (page 13)

DISGUISED. The numbers that repeat are two 7s, two 3s, and two 2s. These total 24. Q is therefore worth 10. S is worth 2, so D is worth 7. This means that E = 14 - 10, or 4. The remaining unidentified repeated number is 3, so I is 3. Therefore G is 9 and U is 1.

Miss You Already (page 13)

A. The missing number is 19. This sequence is actually 2 sequences combined:

13 14 15 16 17 18 _19_

19 17 15 13 11 9

B. The missing number is 1. Starting with the first and last numbers, and working toward the middle, each pair of numbers totals 25.

C. The missing number is 279,936. $0^1=1$; $1^2=1$; $2^3=8$; $3^4=81$; $4^5=1,024$; $5^6=15,625$; and $6^7=279,936$.

Star Power (page 14)

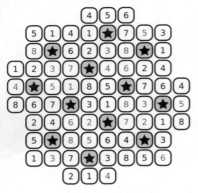

Number Crossword (page 15)

		4	3	2
	8	7	6	5
5	5		6	6
6	5	4	3	
2	8	9		

Go Figure (page 16)

Answers may vary.

						28
9	6	2	1	4	3	25
5	2	2	4	1	7	21
3	7	6	2	3	4	25
2	4	9	5	3	1	24
1	7	2	5	4	2	21
6	1	5	4	8	3	27

26 27 26 21 23 20 29

The Whys and Wherefores (page 16)

The value of Y could be from 2 to 6.

Cross Count (page 17)

S$_1$H$_8$A$_1$G$_7$	17
P$_7$O$_6$R$_9$E$_5$	27
A$_1$S$_1$E$_5$A$_1$	8
N$_5$E$_5$A$_1$R$_9$	20
14	20	16	22

Sudoku (page 18)

2	4	1	9	5	6	8	3	7
7	9	3	8	1	4	6	2	5
6	5	8	2	7	3	1	9	4
1	2	4	7	9	5	3	6	8
3	7	5	1	6	8	2	4	9
8	6	9	4	3	2	5	7	1
9	3	7	5	2	1	4	8	6
4	1	6	3	8	7	9	5	2
5	8	2	6	4	9	7	1	3

Twenty-four Jumble (page 18)

$3 \times 9 - 3 = 24$

Perfect Score (page 19)

1 + 30 + 69 = 100

Number Crossword (page 19)

4	4	1	
4	6	9	1
	8	3	8
	6	5	4

Figuring Fast Food (page 20)

$2.75. If a burger and fries cost $3.50, and a small drink and a cookie costs $2.25, then all 4 cost a total of $5. Take away the fries and small drink, which costs $2.25, and the remaining burger and cookie cost $2.75.

Greedy Gears (page 21)

Crypto-Logic (page 22)

SIMPLE. If T is 12 then P - 1 = 4. So P is 5. Therefore O is 10, and S is 8. 10 - S = M so M is 2. So I is 1. Therefore E is 3, and L is 6.

Calcu-doku (page 22)

4	3	1	2
3	2	4	1
1	4	2	3
2	1	3	4

Number Square (page 23)

3	5	7
9	1	4
8	2	6

Vex-a-gon (page 23)

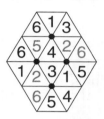

Digital Sudoku (page 24)

1	2	6	5	4	3
5	4	3	1	2	6
6	3	1	2	5	4
2	5	4	3	6	1
4	1	5	6	3	2
3	6	2	4	1	5

How Much? (page 24)

Jacques is the goalie, and he made $8 million.

Lefty is the pitcher, and he made $10 million.

Peydey is the quarterback, and he made $12 million.

LeBucks is the point guard, and he made $14 million.

31

Hashi (page 25)

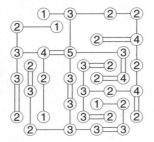

1-2-3 (page 27)

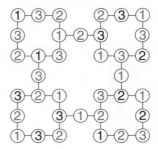

Odd-Even Logidoku (page 26)

6	8	3	2	5	4	7	9	1
5	2	4	7	9	1	3	6	8
7	9	1	8	6	3	2	4	5
9	6	8	3	1	7	4	5	2
3	5	7	6	4	2	8	1	9
4	1	2	5	8	9	6	7	3
1	7	9	4	2	8	5	3	6
2	3	6	1	7	5	9	8	4
8	4	5	9	3	6	1	2	7

Cross-Math (page 26)

8	×	1	+	9	=	17
+		+		+		
4	×	3	+	6	=	18
-		-		÷		
7	×	2	+	5	=	19
=		=		=		
5		2		3		